David Mamet was born in Chicago in 1947. He studied at
Goddard College in Vermont and at the Neighbor...
Playhouse School of Theater in New York. He ... a
Goddard College, the Yale School of Drama and New York
University, and lectures at the Atlantic Theater Company,
of which he is a founding member. He is the author of the
plays *The Cryptogram, Oleanna, Speed-the-Plow, Glengarry Glen
Ross, American Buffalo* and *Sexual Perversity in Chicago*. His films
include, as screenwriter, *The Postman Always Rings Twice, The
Verdict, The Untouchables, The Edge, Wag the Dog* and *The Life of
David Gale*, and as writer/director, *House of Games, Homicide,
Things Change, The Spanish Prisoner* and *State and Main*. He is
also the author of children's books, four books of essays, two
novels, and two books on drama, *True and False* and *Three
Uses of the Knife*. His plays have won the Pulitzer Prize and
the Obie Award.

David Mamet

Romance

Methuen Drama

Published by Methuen 2005

1 3 5 7 9 10 8 6 4 2

First published in the United Kingdom
in 2005 by Methuen Publishing Limited
11–12 Buckingham Gate
London SW1E 6LB

Copyright © 2005 David Mamet

David Mamet has asserted his rights under
the Copyright, Designs and Patents Act, 1988,
to be identified as the author of this work

Methuen Publishing Limited Reg. No. 3543167

A CIP catalogue record for this book is available from
the British Library

ISBN 0 413 77558 5

Typeset by Country Setting, Kingsdown, Kent
Printed and bound in Great Britain by
Bookmarque Ltd, Croydon, Surrey

Caution

Romance

Romance received its European premiere on 6 September 2005 at the Almeida Theatre, London, presented in association with Ron Kastner, Mark Rubinstein and Sonia Friedman Productions. The cast was as follows:

Judge	John Mahoney
Defendant	Nigel Lindsay
Prosecutor	Nicholas Woodeson
Defence Attorney	Colin Stinton
Bailiff	Geff Francis
Bernard	Paul Ready
Doctor	Nick Sampson
Direction	Lindsay Posner
Design	Peter McKintosh
Lighting	Neil Austin
Sound	Matthew Berry
Casting	Maggie Lunn
US Casting	Jim Carnahan

The world premiere of *Romance* was presented by the Atlantic Theater Company, New York City, on 24 February 2005.

Scene One

A courtroom.

The **Judge** *is on the bench. The* **Defendant** *is being interrogated by a* **Prosecutor**. *The* **Defence Attorney** *sits at the defence bench. A* **Bailiff** *stands at the side.*

Prosecutor Who is the person in the hotel room?

Defendant I have no idea.

Prosecutor You were there. You were seen there.

Defendant By whom?

Prosecutor Just answer the question, please.

Defendant Then please may I be addressed with one?

Pause.

Would you please address me with a question?

Pause.

'You were seen there' is not a question.

Prosecutor Just answer the question as you've been directed.

Defendant Well, you ask the questions, and I will attempt to answer them.

Defence Attorney Your Honor, my client is endeavoring . . .

Prosecutor Excuse me?

Defence Attorney . . . to respond to the questions.

Prosecutor Oh, *please* . . .

Defence Attorney 'Oh, please'? Your Honor? I must object. This scurrilous, this sad . . .

Prosecutor May we be spared the . . .

Defence Attorney   This sense of 'weariness', this false, adopted, what is it, a 'charade', a 'vaudeville' . . . ?

Prosecutor   Your Honor, I object, I most strenuously object.

Judge   One moment. May we not have peace?

Pause.

Is that such a strange word? You will forgive me if I pontificate a moment. Will you? If I speak of peace. Is that not the theme of the week?

Prosecutor   It is the theme of the weak. The theme of the strong, Your Honor, if I may, is truth.

Judge   Yes. Thank you. The theme of *this* week. This week's theme. Is it not peace? If not, why are they gathered here? Why are they all come here, if not for peace?

Prosecutor   It is a signal honor, may it please the Court. To welcome them.

Sound of sirens. All listen.

Judge   And there they go. And there they go. The great men. On their way to the Peace Conference . . .

General murmur.

Judge   Mark your calendars, people. It's a Red-Letter Day.

Prosecutor   Indeed it is.

Defence Attorney   Indeed it is.

Judge   It honors our fair city, and it honors us. To see those who have come so far. (*He sneezes.*)

Bailiff   Gezundheit.

Judge   Thank you. And. On our way to work today. The faces. Lining the streets. Perhaps you saw them? This man or that woman. Enemies, perhaps, certainly no more than strangers. Reaching out. Because of our visitors. Yes. Yes. We have strife. But, but, their presence here . . .

Almost sneezes, but holds it.

I'm sorry, did I take my pill?

Bailiff You did, Your Honor.

Judge Thank you. Instructs us, that perhaps, the aim of strife is not victory. No, but simple peace.

All Mmm . . .

Pause.

Judge I'm sorry to've taken your time. Continue.

Pause.

Prosecutor Thank you, Your Honor. Did you contact –

Defendant No.

Prosecutor I must ask you to . . . refrain from interrupting.

Defendant Might I have a glass of water?

Judge Get him a glass of water.

Defendant Thank you, Your Honor.

*The **Bailiff** brings the **Defendant** a glass of water.*

Prosecutor Let me begin again. Did you physically contact a person in Room . . .

Judge And could someone get my pill, please . . . ?

Bailiff Your Honor, you've taken your pill.

Judge I took my pill?

Bailiff Your Honor, yes.

Prosecutor Do you require me to repeat the definition of 'contact'?

Defendant I do not.

Prosecutor I will ask you once again. Do you require me to repeat the definition?

Judge   I took my pill, then why do I have to sneeze?

The **Bailiff** *brings a vial of pills. The* **Judge** *sneezes.*

Bailiff   Gezundheit, Your Honor.

Defence Attorney   Gezundheit.

Judge   Thank you.

Prosecutor   Your Honor, I do not wish to descend to the 'picayune', but as my colleague has wished you Gezundheit, I feel that I must wish you Gezundheit.

Judge   Thank you.

Prosecutor   In fairness to the State.

Judge   Thank you.

Prosecutor   Gezundheit.

Judge   Thank you.

Pause.

Where were we?

Prosecutor (*to the* **Defendant**)   Do you require me to repeat the definition of . . . ?

Judge   Because, I don't know about you people, but I'm moved. Yes. Yes. One becomes callous. But yes, again, we may learn. When we see Two Warring Peoples, Arabs and Jews, an Ancient Enmity. Opposed since Bible times, I'm sorry. I'm moved. Did anyone see the parade?

Defendant   I did, Your Honor.

Prosecutor   I did, Your Honor, too.

Judge   I was moved, I'm sorry. (*He sneezes.*)

All (*pause*)   Gezundheit.

Prosecutor   Alright. You are a chiropodist, are you not?

Defendant   I am not.

Prosecutor   Your Honor, I ask that the defendant be instructed to . . .

Defendant   I am a chiropractor.

Prosecutor   I beg your pardon, I intended to say chiropractor. You are a chiropractor, are you not?

Defendant   I am.

Judge   And I would like to apologize for being late.

Defence Attorney   Not at all, Your Honor.

Judge   You people are giving up *your* time, I see no reason why I should subject you to any further, uh, uh . . .

Prosecutor   Not at all, Your Honor.

Defence Attorney   That's very gracious of you.

Judge   Curiously, I was late because of the parade. I took my *pill*, but I could not remember if I had taken my pill. As they do tend to make one groggy. So I returned to my house. To, to, to take my 'pill', which rendered me late as, on my *leaving* the house, I encountered the parade. (*Pause.*) I would have been on time if not for the . . .

Pause.

Defence Attorney   Of course, Your Honor.

Judge   Parade. A policeman. *Stopped* them, for a moment. Just to let me through. He didn't have to do that. He had no idea who I am. Call me a weepy old fool.

Pause.

Prosecutor   Alright. When, could you tell me, please, did you last leave the country?

Defendant   Thank you, Your Honor, for the water.

Judge   I need a glass of water, too.

Bailiff *goes for the glass of water.*

Prosecutor   When did you last leave the country?

Judge   I have to take my pill.

Defendant   *This* country?

Judge   I mentioned the parade.

Prosecutor   Indeed, Your Honor did.

Pause.

Judge   Good.

Prosecutor (*to the* **Defendant**)   Is this your signature?

Defendant (*pause*)   I do not know.

Prosecutor   Does it appear to be your signature?

Pause.

Defendant   I don't know.

Judge   So many people. But, I suppose, that's the *nature* of a parade.

A slight murmur of appreciation.

Prosecutor   Surely you know if it's your signature?

Defendant   I . . .

Prosecutor   Is it *like* your signature?

Defendant   Yes.

Prosecutor   In what way?

Pause.

Defendant   It is written . . . it is written similarly to my signature . . .

Prosecutor   It *is* . . .

Pause.

Defendant   I just said so.

Prosecutor   Similarly to your signature. Fine.

Judge   I guess what I am trying to say is this: we get caught up in the 'form', the law, religion, nationality . . . uh . . . skin color. And then, and then, *miraculously*, *miraculously*, now and then, and by the grace of God, we are free. And see, that, underneath. We love each other.

All   Mmm.

Judge   That two world leaders, steeped in *enmity* . . .

Pause.

Prosecutor   Momentous days, Your Honor.

Defence Attorney   Yes, momentous days, Your Honor.

Judge   I think we can so stipulate.

*Laughter from the two **Attorneys**.*

Judge   And I'm not even Jewish . . .

Prosecutor   On the date in question . . .

Judge   You know, I'd like to take that back. I don't even know why I say 'not even', I believe a more 'neutral' expression might have been: 'And I'm not Jewish.'

Pause.

Proceed.

Prosecutor   How does this signature differ from your signature?

Pause.

Defendant   I don't know.

Prosecutor   You said this resembles your signature in part.

Defendant   I did . . .

Prosecutor   Let me *suggest* to you that I would like you to *inform* me in what way this *differs* from your signature.

Pause.

Defendant   I don't know.

Prosecutor   Then would you say they are the same?

Judge   One moment.

Prosecutor   Yes, Your Honor.

Judge   The pills, I believe, have made me 'drowsy', and I beg your pardon, but. If you'd indulge me: what is the difference between a chiropodist and a chiropractor?

Defendant   A chiropractor, aligns the spine, to create both physical and spiritual harmony.

Judge   And the other fellow?

Defendant   He rubs people's feet.

Judge   For *pay*?

Pause.

Defendant   Yes, Your Honor.

Judge   And you're *which*, now?

Defence Attorney   Your Honor, my client is a chiropractor.

Pause.

Prosecutor   Alright. Do you deny this is your signature?

Defendant   May I have a moment?

He goes into conference with the **Defence Attorney**.

Judge (*to* **Bailiff**)   Jimmy: is it hot in here?

Bailiff   Would Your Honor like the window opened?

Defendant   I can neither deny nor affirm that signature is mine.

Prosecutor   What would assist you?

Pause. Conference between **Defendant** *and* **Defence Attorney**.

Judge   No, no, I think I prefer the heat to the noise.

Defendant   I cannot say that there is any *thing* which would assist me.

Judge   Because it's *noisy*. Well it's *noisier* because of the *parade* . . .

Pause.

So much of life is a choice, between the lesser of two evils.

Pause.

I suppose that's what I'm *here* for . . .

Dutiful laughter. Pause.

They rub people's feet for 'pay'?

Defendant   Yes. Your Honor.

Judge   Ah, well . . .

Defendant   I quite agree, Your Honor.

Pause.

Prosecutor   I have here a document, which bears your signature. Do you recognize it?

Defendant   It is a check.

Prosecutor   It is one of your checks. It bears your account number. Your name is printed on it. It was signed by you. Do you . . . and it was honored by the bank. Do you acknowledge it to be your signature? Let me put it differently: do you *dispute* it?

Defendant   May I have a rest?

Prosecutor   Do you dispute it? A check. In the amount of this credit card bill. The bill contains a charge for two air fares. Here is the credit card slip. Signed by you.

Judge   You know . . .

Prosecutor   Your Honor, if I might continue, here is the check signed by you. Both signatures were accepted as valid, one by the travel agency, one by the bank. You disputed neither.

Defendant   I might have gone to Hawaii.

Prosecutor   Ah.

Defendant   But that would not be said to be leaving the country.

Prosecutor   Perhaps you would confine yourself to responding to my questions.

Defendant   It is not leaving the country.

Prosecutor   What is not?

Defendant   A trip to Hawaii.

Prosecutor   You *went* to Hawaii?

Defendant   I did not say that.

Prosecutor   Yes you did.

Defendant   But . . . but . . . might I . . . might I finish? *Might* I finish? Might I have an opportunity to *explain* myself? Do you think? In the midst of this, this . . . in the midst of this inquisition?

Pause.

Do you think? As one human being, speaking to another? I might *do* that?

Prosecutor   Might I suggest if you wish to have the proceedings terminated happily and quickly you might do well to respond to my questions? Now. Did you, in the months in question, leave the *mainland*?

Defendant (*pause*)   I do not recall.

Judge   What?

Prosecutor   He does not recall.

Judge   I'm sorry. I'm sorry. My mind was drifting. He does not recall what?

Prosecutor   If he left the mainland.

Judge   Isn't that something one would know?

Prosecutor   I quite agree, Your Honor.

Judge   Don't you know, son, if you left the mainland?

Defendant   I don't recall, sir.

Prosecutor   What would assist you?

Defendant   I don't know.

Prosecutor   Let me understand you: you do not know if . . .

Defendant   I don't know. Yes.

Prosecutor   If you left the mainland?

Judge   The mainland of what, please?

Pause.

Prosecutor   Of, of the continent.

Judge   And he doesn't *know* that . . . ?

Defendant   That is right.

Pause.

Prosecutor   Do you *feel*. Let me put it differently: in your *experience* in this . . . is such a recollection within the abilities of a reasonable man?

Pause.

Defendant   I don't understand.

Prosecutor   I withdraw the question. And I ask you at this point if you are suggesting mental incapacity.

Defence Attorney   Your Honor . . .

Prosecutor   Do you suggest your inability to retain a date, or movement on your part, over the course of a year, do you put it forth as evidence of mental incapacity? Yes or no.

Defence Attorney   Your Honor, please, this is unnecessary. This is . . .

Defendant   If I asked you −

Prosecutor   I beg your pardon, I am not the issue here.

Defendant   If I asked *anyone*. (*Pause.*) Some . . . some. Would have a . . . how can you say it is mental incapacity? That's, that's, that's. Vicious. To offer that, excuse me, sir, that's . . . *Anyone* might. Misremember, or . . .

Judge   That's correct . . .

Prosecutor   Yes?

Judge   Yes, in a busy life . . .

Prosecutor   . . . anyone might disremember . . .

Defendant   . . . or have difficulty remembering . . .

Prosecutor   Yes . . .

Defendant   . . . a *date*, or . . . that, that . . . that is, just . . .

Prosecutor   You're saying that's human nature?

Defendant   Absolutely.

Judge   That is human nature. Fellas. Just this morning, I, uh . . .

Pause.

People forget.

Prosecutor   You've said that you have difficulty with your memory. That's right. It is human nature. Yes. It is. How does one deal with it?

Judge   Is it hot in here?

Judge *lays his head down on the desk.*

Defendant   One, one has, they have agendas, or . . .

Prosecutor   People have difficulty remembering, so they have agendas?

Defendant   Yes.

Prosecutor   Which they would trust more than their recollections?

Defendant   Yes. That is the purpose of them.

Prosecutor   That they would prefer notations on a scrap of paper?

Defendant   As you know.

Judge (*lifts his head up*)   If we could move it along, gentlemen, I am not feeling too . . .

Prosecutor   If it please the Court.

Judge   I find I'm not feeling too well.

Prosecutor   With the Court's pardon, if I might, the one instant . . .

Judge   I found that my mind was drifting. That's not like me.

Defendant   Many times, Your Honor, sitting for long periods stresses the spine and induces a decrease in the fluid of the dural matter which may cause lapses in attention.

Judge   Yes, you bet, but, in truth? I thought I'd step down, just . . . just . . . (*He sneezes.*)

Bailiff   Gezundheit, Your Honor . . .

Judge   Thank you. To be a part of the parade. Do you know, just to be a part of it. I wonder if the pollen in the elm trees near the consulate exacerbated my attack.

Defendant   Is it elm to which Your Honor is allergic?

Judge   Do they have 'pollen'? I suppose they'd have to, as they're 'trees'. They're 'trees', right, Jimmy? They're 'trees'? Right, '*elm trees*'.

Bailiff   Your Honor?

Judge   Well, they say tomatoes are a fruit.

Prosecutor   Might we, with respect to the Court, confine and limit our attention to the . . .

Judge   Quite quite right. I beg your pardon.

Prosecutor   I will be brief.

Judge   It stuck in my mind, because I have an allergy to pollen.

Prosecutor   I . . .

Judge   I'm not feeling well, and, in fact, I think I'd like to call a recess.

Prosecutor   One moment, Your Honor, please, is all I ask.

Judge   *Is* there, um, pollen, in the elm?

Prosecutor   I don't know, Your Honor.

Judge   Or is that just a thing we associate with 'bees'?

Pause.

Prosecutor (*to* **Defendant**)   I ask you to turn your attention to this document, and to identify it for me, please.

Pause.

Would you identify it for me, please? Is this your agenda? For the year in question?

Defendant   Yes.

Prosecutor   It is your name?

Defendant   Yes.

Prosecutor   Is this your *handwriting*?

Pause.

Defendant   I . . .

Prosecutor   Who is the person in the hotel?

Defendant   I . . .

Prosecutor   Is it 'B'?

Defendant   I didn't . . .

Prosecutor   Is that a man's name?

Defendant   I . . .

Prosecutor   'B'. Does that stand for the name of a *man*?

Defendant   I . . .

Prosecutor   Is this your handwriting? Here. Would you look here, please? Here. Would you read that sign, please?

Pause.

Would you read it, please?

Defendant   It appears to . . .

Prosecutor   What is your problem? Would you read the sign?

Defendant   It appears to . . .

Pause.

Prosecutor   What is the sign?

Defendant   I cannot . . .

Prosecutor   Is it the letter 'B'?

Defendant   It appears to, I . . .

Prosecutor   What *follows* it?

Pause.

Defendant   It is a symbol.

Prosecutor   And what is the symbol?

Pause.

Defendant   An arrow.

Prosecutor   An arrow. What is it pointing to?

Defendant   It app . . .

Prosecutor   Don't tell me what it appears to be. What is it? Is it not the letter 'H'? And are you going to tell me that it is a 'ladder' or a 'football goal'? It is the letter H. The phrase or ideogram: 'B', arrow, H, or perhaps, Hawaii . . .

Defence Attorney   Objection.

Prosecutor   . . . or: 'B' to Hawaii. Is that correct?

Defence Attorney   Objection.

Defendant   That is your understanding.

Prosecutor   Indeed it is.

Judge *sneezes.*

Defence Attorney   Gezun . . .

Prosecutor   One moment . . . Indeed it is, and the symbol following?

Defendant   I . . . .

Prosecutor   A 'love heart'? And: following that?

Defence Attorney   Your Honor . . .

Prosecutor   Is it a rabbit?

Defendant   I . . .

Prosecutor   Is it a rabbit in quotes? Sir . . .

Judge *begins sneezing again.*

Prosecutor   . . . with a Happy Face? What is the happy rabbit a symbol of?

Defendant   I, um, Your Honor . . . ?

Defence Attorney   Your Honor, if I might suggest . . .

The **Judge** *continues sneezing.*

Defendant   I don't think it's a rabbit . . . Your Honor, I . . .

Judge   Did I take my pill?

Prosecutor   ARE YOU GOING TO SIT THERE AND TELL ME THAT IS NOT A RABBIT . . . ? YOU LYING, SICK, PERJURED . . .

Defence Attorney   Objection . . .

Judge (*sneezing*)   Gentlemen, gentlemen, may we not have peace?

Defendant   I, I, I . . .

Prosecutor   Are you going to tell me that is not a *rabbit*?

Defence Attorney   Objection, objection, objection.

Judge   May we not have peace?

Defendant   I, I, I . . .

Prosecutor   Are you going to tell me that is not a *rabbit*?

Defence Attorney   It doesn't look like a rabbit to me.

Prosecutor   Not everyone has the equal capacity to draw a rabbit.

Defence Attorney (*of the drawing*)   What are those?

Prosecutor   Ears. Those are ears, those are its ears, they're rabbit ears.

Defence Attorney   No one could draw a rabbit that inexpertly, Your Honor . . .

Judge   Achoo.

Defence Attorney   No one, no one . . .

Prosecutor   Not everyone, Your Honor, has the God-given ability to draw a rabbit.

Judge   Achoo.

Prosecutor   I can and will present a cavalcade of expert witnesses . . .

Judge   I don't think my prescription is working . . .

Prosecutor   Your Honor, one moment.

Judge   ACHOO ACHOO ACHOO.

Prosecutor   Expert witnesses, who cannot draw a rabbit.

Judge   Ah, shit, I think I'm going to have to lay down.

Scene Two

Small conference room. The **Defendant** *and the* **Defence Attorney**.

Pause.

Defence Attorney   Well, you know, it looked like a fucken rabbit to *me*. I asked you. Didn't I ask you? Not To Get Up On The Stand? Did I ask you that?

Defendant   I . . .

Defence Attorney   It looked like a fucken rabbit to me.

Defendant   What if I was not there?

Defence Attorney   Ah hell, where?

Defendant   In Hawaii.

Defence Attorney   I don't know any more.

Defendant   Well, I'm paying you to know. So just . . .

Defence Attorney   You're paying me to give you my advice. And my advice was not to get up on the stand, you *got* up . . .

Defendant   Well, I got up on the stand . . .

Defence Attorney   You got up there, and made a fool, not only of yourself, but –

Defendant   I got up on the stand, because, because I feel –

Defence Attorney   And then he asked you about the rabbit. 'What were you doing in Hawaii with a happy rabbit?'

Defendant   What if I was not there?

Defence Attorney   Were you there?

Defendant   Would you follow me, please?

Defence Attorney   If you were not there. One would be hard pressed to account for the for the rabbit and all. 'B', arrow, love heart, to Hawaii, rabbit. If you were not

there. Anyone 'reading' them. Would ask you. If you were
not there, would ask for your 'story'.

Defendant   For My Story.

Defence Attorney   Yes.

Defendant   But. (*Pause.*) But would you . . . yes, I know,
I understand . . . But. As an 'exercise'.

Defence Attorney   We have so little . . .

Defendant   Please. As a, as, as a *hypothetical instance*. Please.
In which, alright. Alright?

Pause.

Defence Attorney   Alright.

Defendant   In which the facts seemed to be. Seemed to
be . . .

Defence Attorney   Do you know, and now he calls a
recess. And I'm never going to be able to get home –

Defendant   I . . .

Defence Attorney   – with the parade.

Defendant   The point.

Defence Attorney   The point. The point is not . . .

Defendant   Please . . .

Defence Attorney   May I finish: the point is not what you
ad –

Defendant   . . . I understand.

Defence Attorney   – what you *admit*.

Defendant   I understand that.

Defence Attorney   But –

Defendant   I underst –

Defence Attorney   But, please let me, what a reasonable
person must infer from the facts.

Defendant I understand that.

Defence Attorney If you understand, then I am baffled by . . .

Defendant I'm asking, as a hypothetical instance.

Defence Attorney I, I, I, I feel that I am being remiss in my duties.

Defendant A hypothetical instance where . . .

Defence Attorney We have so little time.

Defendant If, if we postulate.

Defence Attorney To indulge in . . . Listen to me –

Defendant I . . .

Defence Attorney To indulge in. Please, alright, I know, believe me, no, I *realize* that, to you, much of the proceedings must seem, they must seem to you *arbitrary*, and . . .

Bailiff *enters with a newspaper.*

Bailiff You fellas want lunch?

Defendant If we posit a hypothetical instance where . . .

Defence Attorney You were in Hawaii. November Tenth, of last year. B, arrow, love heart, Hawaii, laughing rabbit. You were there. How in the *fuck* are you not going to have been there – ?

Defendant By providing an alternative.

Defence Attorney To where you were?

Defendant To, to a way of 'looking' at it.

Defence Attorney Alright, then, after the mumbo jumbo, what is the alternative?

Defendant My understanding is, at that point, that is *your* job.

Defence Attorney And my job is?

Defendant   To, to frame an alternative . . . to present to the Judge . . .

Defence Attorney   A *lie* . . . ? (*Pause*.) *A LIE?*

Bailiff   Anybody want to see the paper?

Defendant   Oh, Lord, oh Lord, now I *am* in trouble . . . now I am, truly, truly fucked. Oh, God, oh, God . . . You don't want to *lie?*

Defence Attorney   If you would let me do my job . . .

Defendant   Why did you go to *law* school? If you don't want to *lie?*

Defence Attorney (*pause*)   I . . .

Bailiff (*looking at the paper*)   Big doings at the Peace Conference . . .

Defendant   You're fired.

Pause.

Defence Attorney   I fear you don't understand.

Defendant   You're f-f-f . . .

Defence Attorney   Can you suppose that another representation would be more to your taste?

Defendant   I don't know.

Defence Attorney   Well, I *do* know. YOU'RE *GUILTY*. DO YOU UNDERSTAND?

Defendant   I AM NOT GUILTY UNTIL A DULY CONSTITUTED COURT . . .

Defence Attorney   What BULLSHIT. WHAT UTTER CRAP. YOU MAKE ME SICK. YOU MAKE ME ASHAMED. YOU MAKE ME, I'M FILLED WITH CONTEMPT, WITH, *FUCK*, CONTEMPT, WITH LOATHING, AND YOU SIT UP THERE, GUILTY AS SIN, CRIMINAL, SICK, PERVERTED, AND I'M –

Defendant   Wait one moment . . .

Defence Attorney   – trying, trying, somehow to . . .

Defendant   I'm paying you . . .

Defence Attorney   A *pittance*, for what I go through?
Forced to sit *next* to you, you SICK FUCK, day after day,
supporting you; nodding at your infantile hypocrisies. This sick
Talmudic, Jewish . . . (*Pause.*) Ohmigod.

Defendant   Aha.

Defence Attorney   I . . . I . . . I must, *most* humbly, *most*
humbly. *Beg.* Your forgiveness. My speech has run away with
me, I . . . I was to take my son, my son Tommy. To the
Church youth hockey game today, and it is. A *particularly*
anxious time. As, as I am divorced, I see him seldom. And
these outings, and the time we spend together. Are *precious*
to us, and I am somewhat distraught. At the *probability* that
I will be late, and, and I can but most sincerely Beg Your
Pardon.

Pause.

Defendant   I accept your apology.

Defence Attorney   Thank you. That is gracious and
generous of you.

Defendant   I understand your anxiety.

Defence Attorney   Thank you.

Defendant   I know that you are a religious man . . .

Defence Attorney   Yes, I am . . .

Defendant   . . . that you're taking your son to a Church
function . . .

Defence Attorney   The youth hockey game . . .

Defendant   . . . and that if you arrived late . . .

Defence Attorney   Yes . . .

Defendant . . . you might have trouble, getting the priest's dick out of your son's ass.

Defence Attorney You fucken kike, you sick, *sick* . . .

Defendant Fuck you.

Defence Attorney . . . Christ-killing Jew, cocksucking *bastard* . . .

Bailiff You fellas want lunch?

Defence Attorney (*to* **Bailiff**) Fuck you, too. Fuck you, too. Fuck the lot of you.

Bailiff Uh . . .

Defence Attorney I'm done, I'm gone, I've been nixed.

Defendant You *are* fired. I say you're fired, and you walk out on me . . .

Defence Attorney Fuck you . . .

Defendant Oh, oh, who's weak now?

Defence Attorney Fuck you. Call me a *liar* . . .

Defendant Is it upset that I used One Little Word?

Defence Attorney You fucking kike.

Defendant Oh, bad man's called him a hypocrite . . .

Defence Attorney You you you you you you you're the fucken hypocrite . . .

Defendant *Am* I . . . ?

Defence Attorney You're fucken well-told right you are, who who who, and who has to suffer for you? (*Pause.*) Uh?

Defendant Oh? *You?*

Bailiff (*looking at paper and holding a pencil*) Prehistoric fish . . .

Defendant Oh – who suffers for my sins . . . ! 'Who gave his Only Begotten Son . . . '?

Pause.

Defence Attorney   What is that supp . . .

Bailiff   Prehistoric fish . . . ten letters . . .

Defendant   You know what that means.

Defence Attorney   No. I'm not sure that I do.

Defendant   No.

Defence Attorney   No. I'm not at all sure that I do.

Defendant   Fuck you.

Bailiff   You guys eaten lunch?

Defence Attorney   Is, that, do I take that to mean . . . ?

Defendant   Fuck you.

Defence Attorney   Fuck me? Fuck *you*, you rug merchant, greasy, hook-nosed, *no*-dick, Christ-killing, son-of-a-bitch sacreligious . . .

Bailiff   The Judge says . . .

Defence Attorney   Fuck the Judge, and fuck *you*, and, and, *you*, you mocky, sheeny *cock*sucker . . . when I've missed taking Little Tommy to Church youth hockey, because I'm stuck in here listening to your snivelling, sick . . .

Defendant   Oh, oh, Little Tommy, again? Limping, when he comes home from Communion, does he . . . ?

Pause.

Defence Attorney   I hope, I hope that the Arabs. Rise in their droves, and drive your people into the sea. Killing the children. Raping their wives and burning down all traces of your two-thousand-year-long sacrilege.

Defendant   Fuck you.

Defence Attorney   And, if there *is* a God. And there is, who died for us, who suffered for mankind, who lives today, and hears all, I pray to that God to hear my plea . . .

Bailiff They're having meatloaf today . . .

Defence Attorney . . . that you, your family, your race . . .

Bailiff . . . on the steam table . . .

Defence Attorney I heard you. And that every sperm, seed, trace, artifact . . .

Defendant If you would be ONE BILLIONTH as persuasive out there . . .

Defence Attorney Fuck you. I'm fired, and you're screwed. Because you're going to prison. Prison. Do you hear? Because the man who (and I am that man) who stood the *remotest* chance of saving your worthless Jew self, the one man . . .

Defendant If you had a fucking clue . . .

Defence Attorney I don't need a clue. I don't *need* a clue. I *needed* you stay off the stand, to . . .

Defendant Submit . . .

Defence Attorney Yes. Submit. At the dentist, do you say, 'They're my teeth: let me help?' YOU NEED TO SUBMIT.

Defendant SUBMIT . . . SUBMIT SUBMIT SUBMIT SUBMIT SUBMIT. God forgive me, what have I done? I hired a goy lawyer! It's like going to a straight hairdresser. And now he wants me to *submit*. You fucken asshole. You brain-dead, white socks, country club, plaid pants, Campbell's soup fucken *sheigetz* Goy. Submit. That's fine. Take the example of Your Lord.

Defence Attorney There I must insist you stop . . .

Defendant Your fairy-tale . . . oooh, they rolled the stone away from the cave . . .

Defence Attorney I've warned you . . .

Defendant While the porridge cooled . . .

Defence Attorney   I'm not warning you again . . .

Defendant   Oh. What will you do? Hitch up your pants and kill every Jew in Europe?

Defence Attorney   It's what you deserve . . .

Defendant   Hitch up your leather pants and gas everybody?

Defence Attorney   . . . a pogrom . . .

Defendant   My very presence here. MY VERY PRESENCE HERE IS A POGROM . . .

Defence Attorney   There it is . . .

Defendant   A pogrom . . .

Defence Attorney   You people can't order a cheese sandwich . . .

Defendant   Fuck you.

Defence Attorney   . . . without mentioning the Holocaust.

Defendant   My people do not *eat* cheese sandwiches.

Defence Attorney   Oh. Oh, what? It isn't 'kosher' . . . ?

Defendant   IT ISN'T *TASTY*. *TASTY*. You mindless Nazi fuck. IT DOESN'T *TASTE* GOOD, AND SO WE DON'T *EAT* IT.

Defence Attorney   IS THAT SO?

Defendant   Yes. Yes. We eat Christian *children*. We bake them in *pies*, just like you have been saying these two thousand years. Your whole dolt, Catholic . . .

Defence Attorney   I'm Episcopalian . . .

Defendant   And what the fuck is *that*? A Catholic with a Volvo . . .

Defence Attorney   Oh, that's charming.

Defendant   Go back to the country club. Drink, fuck each other's wives, and increase the defence budget. Fuck you.

Defence Attorney What's wrong with the defence budget?

Pause.

Defendant What's *wrong* . . . ? What's wrong with the *defence* budget? Are you *serious*?

Bailiff You want lunch?

Defence Attorney What's *wrong*? Yes – with the defence budget, which, among other things, keeps the Israelis and the, the, the, duly constituted Palestinian . . .

Defendant I'll *give* you the Palestinians . . . I'll . . .

Defence Attorney Oh. What are they? 'Hanky-heads'?

Defendant No . . .

Defence Attorney Savages, who don't deserve . . .

Defendant No.

Defence Attorney 'Sand-Negroes' . . . ?

Bailiff You fellas want lunch?

Defence Attorney I don't want lunch.

Bailiff You might want to eat. Going to be a long afternoon.

Defence Attorney I'm not hungry.

Bailiff I was you, I'd eat. What do you eat?

Defendant What do you mean?

Bailiff I mean 'What do you eat?'

Defendant I eat 'food'. What do you mean?

Defence Attorney He meant, is there anything you don't eat?

Defendant There's lots of things that I eat. If they're food I eat them. Why do you ask?

Defence Attorney He asked out of politeness, because you're Jewish.

Defendant How would he know that?

Defence Attorney You've been shouting 'goy cocksucker' for an hour. What did he think it was? 'Self-loathing'?

Bailiff You fellas see the parade?

Defence Attorney Shouting like some *rug* bazaar . . .

Defendant What does that mean?

Defence Attorney A rug bazaar.

Defendant What does that mean, I know what you said, what does it *mean*?

Defence Attorney It means, it means, my friend . . .

Defendant Don't start in with that.

Defence Attorney With what?

Defendant With the Jew thing: 'my friend'. You goy flunky. Yes, I come from a rug bazaar. Yes. I'm a kike. Yes, I'm a sheeny Jew. I come from the Casbah. I come from the Middle East. Two thousand years ago, when we killed your Lord. That's me. A hook-nosed greasy Jew, who would prefer good, clean logic of a rug . . .

Defence Attorney If . . .

Defendant Shut up . . . of a rug bazaar . . . where each has something . . . to . . .

Defence Attorney If . . .

Defendant You fucken brain-dead, child molester thief *goy* monster, and you tell me Justice? You know what true Justice is?

Defence Attorney No, please tell me.

Defendant It is the rug bazaar.

Defence Attorney Ah ha . . .

Defendant You want to solve the evils of the world? You want to know how? By reducing the discussion, to a simple human need. Instead of screaming at me, standing me up in front of the Prosecutor of Judea . . . and, by the way, he was Jewish . . .

Defence Attorney   Who?

Defendant   Christ.

Defence Attorney   Christ Jesus? Yes. He was a Jew. Yes. I affirm that.

Defendant   Sporting of you.

Defence Attorney   No, I'm sick of it. I'm sick of listening to you, malign my faith.

Defendant   Fuck you.

Defence Attorney   From a chiropractor? From a 'chiropractor' . . . ?

Defendant   My profession, sir . . .

Defence Attorney   And now I've missed the hockey game . . .

Defendant   My profession, sir . . .

Defence Attorney   Fuck your profession . . .

Defendant   . . . was alleviating suffering when doctors dwelt in caves.

Defence Attorney   Through rubbing people's feet . . .

Defendant   No, actually, through realignment, of the *spine* . . .

Defence Attorney   Oh, bullshit.

Defendant   . . . realignment of the spine, excuse me, yes, which, even in the most obstinate cases . . .

Defence Attorney   Oh, *please* . . .

Defendant   . . . brings about reversal of disease, well-*being*, right *thinking*, and . . . ohmigod . . .

Defence Attorney   What?

Defendant   OHMIGOD.

Defence Attorney   *What?*

Defendant   *I KNOW HOW TO BRING PEACE TO THE MIDDLE EAST!*

Scene Three

The **Prosecutor** *is giving a speech to what appears to be an empty room.*

Prosecutor   In every time, this one or that, has introduced a New Thing. Never Before Seen Upon The Earth. And called it Bohemia. Radicalism. Freedom, this doctrine, of licence, this notion that we are above the law. Based upon what? This brave announcement? The individual's sentiment of being Chosen. Laws, my friend, and laws, my neighbors, however, came into being as we learned, at long, hard cost, and both to our chagrin and to our education, that we cannot *trust* our senses.

Pause.

Calling crime by the name of 'freedom'. And by any other name than that set down in law. But the law will find you. That which first was a reminder comes again as a demand – a correction. For I, for you, no less than that man tempted, fallen, and now brought before you, answers to the law. And you who judge him must be still, and ask of yourselves honest and hard dedication. To that ideal, which *alone* can guide us – and it is a tree of life. To those who hold fast to it. (*Pause.*) What do you think? (*Pause.*) Tell me truly. (*Pause.*) Go on.

Pause.

Bernard, *a young fellow, rises from the couch, where he has been hidden.*

Bernard I don't know.

Prosecutor ... *Oh God.*

Bernard I just. I don't know.

Prosecutor Oh God.

Bernard I ...

Prosecutor Spare me. *Spare* –

Bernard I ...

Prosecutor Please. Please. *Spare* me your pity.

Bernard It may, will you wait a second ... It may be, it's *possible* that ...

Prosecutor Please ...

Bernard Will you let me finish? It's *possible* that it's just a bit too strong.

Prosecutor What in the *world* can that mean?

Pause.

Bernard I ...

Prosecutor What can you mean to tell me, that it is 'TOO STRONG'?

Bernard For *me*. Too strong for *me*. At this *point.*

Prosecutor No, no, *how* can it ... how can it be Too Strong?

Bernard I ...

Prosecutor Could I, do you think, would you just, for godsake, say that you don't *like* it?

Bernard No, that's not the case.

Prosecutor It *is* the case.

Pause.

Bernard I ...

Prosecutor (*simultaneously*)   Do you have any notion how *humiliating* this is . . . ?

Pause.

Bernard   I . . .

Prosecutor (*simultaneously*)   . . . to indulge in this *hypocrisy*.

Bernard   I . . .

Pause.

Prosecutor   Well, fine, fine. What would you change?

Bernard   I . . .

Prosecutor   What?

Bernard   I *do* like it.

Prosecutor   That was not my question.

Bernard   I . . .

Prosecutor   Would you, would you please, for the love of God? Please. (*Pause.*) Would you *please*? (*Pause.*) For God's sake? (*Pause.*) You follow me . . . ?

Bernard   I . . .

Prosecutor   Would you just leave me alone for a while? (*Pause.*) Do you think?

Bernard   I'm sorry if I hurt you.

Prosecutor   I'm sure that you are. (*Pause.*) I know that you are.

Bernard   I . . .

Prosecutor   Seriously.

Pause.

Bernard   Thank you.

Pause.

Prosecutor   If I could just be *alone* for a while.

Bernard *starts to speak.*

Prosecutor   Yes. No. I know. (*Pause.*) *Thank* you. (*Pause.*)
Thank you. I mean that seriously. I just want to be alone.

Bernard   I don't want you to be angry with me.

Prosecutor   I'm not angry with you.

Bernard   I'm so sorry.

Prosecutor   I'm not angry.

Bernard   I . . .

Prosecutor   It's alright. I'm, I'm, I'm a little up . . .

Bernard   No. Truly. I . . . I humbly beg your . . .

Prosecutor   WOULD YOU GET THE FUCK OUT OF
HERE AND LEAVE ME ALONE? HAVE YOU ANY
IDEA HOW HUMILIATING THIS IS . . . ?

Bernard   I . . .

Prosecutor   Bullshit. *Bullshit.*

A smoke alarm sounds from offstage. A take to it.

Bernard   I . . .

Prosecutor   *Bullshit.* It's about *you.* It's all about *you.* How
contrite you are. How little you demand, how . . .

Alarm beeps twice.

Bernard   You . . .

Prosecutor   *No. Don't* say that.

Bernard   You don't . . .

Prosecutor   Yes. I do. This is, no. This is *not* 'one of those
things'. And I won't have it. Do you hear? What? Have
I 'hurt your *feelings*'?

Bernard   I . . .

Alarm sounds agian.

Prosecutor   I'm losing you. I'm losing you. I know it.
Don't lie to me. Please please please, just tell me the truth.
For once, as if I were man enough to hear it.

Alarm.

Bernard   You are man enough to hear it.

Prosecutor   I am?

Bernard   Yes.

Alarm.

Prosecutor   To hear it.

Bernard   Yes.

Alarm beeps continuously. Smoke billows in.

Prosecutor (*spoken over alarm*)   To hear what? (*Pause.*) What
are we talking about? Oh, my God, now I am lost. What
are we talking about? My whole world is a mass of pain.
The ground is shifting under my feet, and I know, for the
first time, I know what they mean. When they say, uh . . .
uh . . . (*Pause.*) Uh . . . what the fuck is that?

Phone rings as **Prosecutor** *storms off.* **Bernard** *answers the
phone.*

Bernard (*on phone*)   Hello? He's in the kitchen. (*Pause.*)
Because the stew is burning is why. Because I forgot to turn
it down. (*Pause.*) Because I'm a dunce, alright? (*Pause.*) Well,
I was born that way. I suppose it's genetic. (*Pause.*) A lot of
people say that.

Beeping ends. **Prosecutor** *re-enters.*

Bernard   There's a phone call for you.

Prosecutor   Fuck you.

Bernard   Fuck you, too.

Prosecutor   And fuck you, *too.*

Bernard   And fuck *you.*

Prosecutor (*into phone*)   Hello. No. It's a fine time. It's swell.
What do you want? I can't talk to you. Tell it to me
tomorrow. Well, what is it you're going to *tell* me tomorrow?
(*Pause.*) To suspend the prosecution? Why?

Bernard   The stew is burnt.

Prosecutor   Fuck you. (*Pause. Into phone.*) *TO DROP THE
CHARGES? YOUR GUY IS AS GUILTY AS THE LORD
KNOWS HOW TO MAKE HIM.* (*Pause.*) I don't *want* to give
him a cont . . . I don't *want* to give him a continuance *either*.
Why should I give him a continuance? (*Pause.*) *TO TAKE
PART IN THE PEACE PROCESS?*

Bernard   Tell him to go with God.

Prosecutor   Fuck you.

Bernard   Fuck you, too.

Prosecutor   And fuck you, *too*. You little two-bit piece of
fucking INTELLECTUAL FLUFF.

Bernard   Oh, oh, oh, did you marry me for my *mind*?

Prosecutor   Fuck you.

Bernard   So that we could discuss *Proust*? Was that what
had you GLUED TO THE SMALL LEATHER GOODS
COUNTER AT SAKS, DAY AFTER DAY?

Prosecutor   Fuck you.

Bernard   *Mooning . . . ?*

Prosecutor (*into phone*)   He's going to bring peace *how . . . ?*

Bernard   I'm like, hey, buy a *wallet . . .*

Prosecutor   Fuck you.

Bernard   You cheap *fuck*. Where do you buy your clothes?
The garbage? 'Oh, I love you Bunny.'

Prosecutor   Fuck you.

Bernard   'Please, please, I know I'm fat. I know I have the taste of a Midwestern fucking pet-shop owner . . . I know I'm unworthy of you . . .

Prosecutor   Go on . . .

Bernard   I know I have the contours of a *pear*, and I'm ashamed of myself and I'm no good in *bed*.

Prosecutor   Ah ha . . .

Bernard   'And you're the loveliest thing that I've ever *seen*, and I'm unfit to even gaze upon you,' night after night. Hey, do you like beer? AND MY FRIENDS LOOKED AT YOU LIKE I'D BROUGHT HOME SOME FUCKING *WEATHERMAN*. But, no no no, 'I love you, Bernard. And I'll make a *home* for you, and I'll *protect* you . . . '

Prosecutor   Are you crying? (*Pause.*) Oh, are you crying?

Bernard   Oh, do you think that's some cheap girlish trick?

Prosecutor (*into phone*)   One moment . . .

Bernard   Do you think that's 'unfair'? To have 'feelings'. 'Feelings'? . . . Now I've lost my contact . . .

Bernard *starts crawling around on the floor.*

Prosecutor   Go on . . .

Bernard   . . . I've lost my contact . . .

Prosecutor   Go on . . .

Bernard   I don't want to go on. I want to be left alone.

Prosecutor   Bunny . . .

Bernard   Leave me alone.

Prosecutor   Bunny, I'm over here.

Bernard   I don't care where you are. Go back to your work. Go to your priceless phone call. Go, go on with your 'If it please the Court', sick macho *bullshit*: Mumbo jumbo, habeas gumbo . . . I've lost my contact . . . Put the world in prison. Maybe that will compensate you for your lack of self-esteem. I'm done. I'm done . . . I've burned the roast. *You* clean the fucking pan. I'm sorry for you.

He exits.

Prosecutor (*into phone*)   Hello? (*Pause.*) A friend. What business is it of yours? (*Pause.*) Yeah, I heard you. (*Pause.*) And how would that bring peace to the Middle East? (*Pause.*) Well, too bad, 'cause you get your ass and your client's ass into court tomorrow at ten a.m. (*Pause.*) The Judge is not sick, he has hay fever. He'll be there and *you* be there . . . I don't give a fuck about the Middle East. Fuck *you*.

Bernard (*re-entering*)   Just two things. One –

Prosecutor   Yes?

Bernard   I'm sorry for you.

Prosecutor   *Are* you?

Bernard   And two – yes, I am. And two: a paste of baking soda and water left in the pan will scrub it clean effortlessly, overnight. Fuck you.

He exits.

Scene Four

The courtroom. Day.

All are present save the **Judge**, *who enters somewhat bedraggled.*

Bailiff   All rise.

Judge   What time is it?

Bailiff   Your Honor, it is nine a.m.

Judge   At night?

Pause.

Bailiff   Your Honor, no.

Judge   Alright.

Defence Attorney   Your Honor, thank you for coming in
early . . . this may, to your ears, be somewhat, more than
unusual. But, I *believe* that we, in these extraordinary
circumstances, have today, an opportunity. You know in
ancient times the Court was, at once, the seat of justice, and
of law, of religion and of political discourse. A 'meeting
house', if you will. A forum, in which the community aired,
exercised, and so *improved* its commerce, morals, and, in this
case, its foreign relations.

Judge   Where am I . . . ?

Pause.

Prosecutor   Your Honor . . .

Judge (*holding up a paper*)   What is this?

Bailiff   Your Honor, it is a request for continuance . . .

Judge   Continuance . . .

Defence Attorney   Your Honor, I think that we possess,
today, an opportunity . . .

Judge   *What* is this . . . ?

Bailiff   Your Honor, it's . . .

Judge   I mean. It's a piece of paper. Right?

Pause.

Defence Attorney   If it please the Court. It is a piece of
paper.

Judge   Is it made from 'wheat'?

Prosecutor   Your Honor, I believe, that it is made from
woodpulp. If it please the Court, you have before you a
request for continuance, on the part of the defence, which
this office most strenuously opposes. On the following grounds.

Defence Attorney   Your Honor. Here, today, in this city.
The representatives of two historically warring powers are
convened. My client and I . . .

Judge   Might I have a glass of water?

Bailiff   There's one before Your Honor.

Judge   Did I take my pill?

Bailiff   I believe, Your Honor, yes . . .

Judge *takes a pill.*

Bailiff   I believe Your Honor did take Your Honor's pill.

Judge   Well, now, I'm sure. Now, uh, now, um, perhaps we can get on with it. I've got to tell you fellas, after a night of no sleep . . . I'm not feeling too well, and . . .

Prosecutor   I opposed, Your Honor, the request, for a continuance . . .

Judge   They changed my prescription.

Prosecutor   Your Honor –

Judge   My first one was putting me to sleep. But I stopped taking it.

Prosecutor   Your Honor, I . . .

Judge   Gimme a pill. One second. Could you give me a pill?

Bailiff   Your Honor, the side effect of overdosing . . .

Judge   What? Do they make me drowsy?

Bailiff   Your Honor, *no*. The *others* made you drowsy. The side effects of *this* pill include, uh, oh . . . (*He reads the label.*)

Judge   We're simply going to have to risk it. *If* justice is to be served. (*He reads.*) What is 'Bunny'?

Prosecutor   I beg Your Honor's pardon, that is a personal note. (*He goes to retrieve the note.*)

Defence Attorney   Your Honor, if I might address the issue . . .

Judge Why does it want to lick you all over?

Pause.

Defence Attorney Your Honor . . . we have. In our city today. The representatives of Two Great Nations . . .

Judge And something's very wrong here.

Defence Attorney What, Your Honor?

Prosecutor Indeed it is. The request, for a continuance, leaving aside the lack of simple human concern for Your Honor's health . . .

Judge I mean with this note. (*Pause.*) There is something quite wrong with this note. You. You received a note, which I find stuck to my motion. Is that true?

Prosecutor (*pause*) Yes, Your Honor.

Judge It's signed 'Bunny'.

Pause.

Prosecutor Yes, Your Honor. It is.

Judge *RABBITS CAN'T WRITE . . .*

Pause.

A phone rings. **Prosecutor** *takes out his cell phone.*

Prosecutor (*into phone*) Don't call me here . . .

Defence Attorney Your Honor, there is a Force For Good, what matter we call it. Some call that force 'God'.

Judge . . . they can't write.

Prosecutor (*into phone*) . . . because I'm at work.

Defence Attorney . . . what matter if we picture, in our mind, an ancient man . . . or woman, with a long white beard. Or if we name it but 'a Power'. We humans are imbued, say 'chemically', if you must, with the disposition to *intuit* such a force. If it leads us toward good. Is it not God?

Prosecutor (*into phone*)   I can't talk now . . .

Judge (*to* **Prosecutor**)   Would you address yourself to that?

Prosecutor   I shall, Your Honor . . . the mention of 'God', in a Court of Law . . .

Judge   I mean, to the rabbit.

Pause.

Prosecutor   The rabbit, Your Honor, is not a legal document.

Judge   Then it should not have been found on my desk.

Prosecutor   It was, unfortunately, Your Honor, stuck to the motion for continuance.

Judge   How?

Prosecutor   With the *au jus*, if you will, of pot roast.

Judge   I can't take any more.

Rising.

Defence Attorney   Your Honor. If Your Honor, please . . . sir. The warring representatives of Israel and Palestine are, today in our city. My client and I, we believe, may have constructed . . .

Defendant   . . . *have* constructed, Your Honor, a method, whereby . . .

Prosecutor (*into phone*)   I said I can't talk now . . .

Defence Attorney   . . . a method, Your Honor, devised by this good man, which, we believe, may bring peace to the Middle East. We crave the Court's indulgence, to be given leave to present him and his method to these two world leaders, who, today, are convened, Your Honor . . . in the name, Your Honor, in the sacred name of peace.

Pause.

Defendant   We think, Your Honor, that this simple procedure could bring about peace.

Prosecutor   What kind of bullshit is this? Your Honor . . . ?

Judge   Don't worry about me . . . they changed my prescription.

Defendant   'Bullshit'?

Judge   The other pills were making me drowsy.

Defendant   Bullshit?

Defence Attorney   Your Honor, the comments of the Prosecutor . . .

Prosecutor   I am in the midst, I beg your pardon, of some, some, some . . . some familial, some . . .

Judge   I didn't know you were married . . .

Prosecutor   And you waltz in here, with this bullshit, *bullshit* rhetoric. Taking in vain the name of peace, of . . .

Defendant   I . . .

Prosecutor   Spawning, this sick, heretic liberal humanistic pagan bullshit, about God and 'many forms' . . .

Defendant   *WHO DIED AND LEFT YOU BOSS?*

Prosecutor   Your Honor . . . ?

Defendant   'Jesus'?

Defence Attorney   Oh. No.

Prosecutor   I beg your pardon?

Defendant   Jesus. A *Jew*. Oy. Are we affronted that He Died on the Cross? And *we* can't mention: Him. Except every third sentence in your bullshit, hypocritical, goy day . . .

Prosecutor   I object . . .

Defendant   In between raping your children, and, and . . .

Prosecutor   Your Honor . . .

Defendant   . . . bombing abortion clinics, and all.

Prosecutor   Your Honor, I must strenuously object to this, vicious, vile . . .

Defendant   You fucking goyim, with 'your wives named Marge'.

Judge   *My* wife is named Marge.

Defendant   Oh, my prophetic soul.

Defence Attorney   Your Honor, what my client intended to say, in referring to 'your wife named Marge' . . .

Prosecutor   What the hell does that mean, 'my prophetic soul'?

Judge   Did I take my pill?

Defendant   It's Shakespeare.

Prosecutor   Oh, bullshit.

Judge   Why is he talking about my wife?

Defendant   Aha, and why don't you like Shakespeare . . . ? Because he was a Jew.

Bailiff   He was a Jew?

Defendant   You bet your boots.

Prosecutor   But that's preposterous.

Defendant   Is it?

Prosecutor   Yes.

Judge   Why is it preposterous?

Defendant   Why is it preposterous?

Prosecutor   It is preposterous because . . . because . . .

Defendant   I'm waiting.

Prosecutor   Because: Shakespeare was not a Jew.

Judge   What was he?

Prosecutor   What was he?

Defendant   Yeah.

Prosecutor   He . . . was a *Christian*.

Defendant   No Christian can write that good.

Judge   What do you say to that? (*Pause.*) Come on, you
want me to do something for you, *you* do something for *me*.

Pause.

Prosecutor   I . . .

Judge   Assuage my ignorance.

Prosecutor   I . . . (*Pause.*) The question before this Court –

Bailiff   He was a fag. I know he was a fag.

Judge   He was a fag . . . ? Shakespeare?

Bailiff   Yup.

Judge   'Shakespeare', who they teach in Schools?

Bailiff   Your Honor, yes.

Prosecutor   Your Honor . . .

Judge   To, to, to, to, to the 'little children'?

Prosecutor   Your Honor, I must object.

Judge   Why, are you a Shakespearean scholar?

Prosecutor   No, Your Honor – (*Big pause for effect.*) I am a
homosexual.

Pause.

Judge   What is it you guys actually 'do'?

Pause.

Prosecutor   Your Honor . . .

Judge   *Seriously* . . .

Long pause.

Defence Attorney Your Honor, the resprespentatives of
two . . .

Judge And could he not have been a Jew *and* a fag?
(*Pause.*) Could he not have been two things . . . ?

Defence Attorney Your Honor, we have, today, an
Historic Opportunity.

Judge And how am I to decide?

Defence Attorney Your Honor?

Judge I mean, 'cause we can't go back, to, uh, Elizabethan
times, and see if, uh, if Shakespeare plucked his eyebrows.

Defence Attorney Your Honor . . .

Judge You know, and if he sometimes 'forgot' to wear
socks with his penny loafers. So: someone has Got To
Decide. (*Pause.*) You see, this is the age-old problem facing
Jurisprudence. This, see, *this* is the thing you never think of.
Oh, I'd like to sit up there, and sentence people to death,
and have a reserved parking space, and so on. It never
occurs to you that there's a *burden* which comes with it.
Nooo. The Burden of Office. That burden is . . . (*Pause.*)
Uh . . . (*Pause.*) It's *uncertainty*.

Pause.

Defence Attorney Your Honor, *tomorrow* the
Representatives of Two Great Powers . . . convened in our
city, will depart, if, *IF*. Your Honor . . .

Judge No *wonder* Solomon cut that baby in half! *You*
would, too! You fucken Goody Two-Shoes. *No*! *Don't* cut it in
half. It's a human *being*! . . . Oh please.

Defence Attorney Your Honor.

Judge *Spare* me . . .

Prosecutor Your Honor . . .

Judge   For the problem – give me another pill – it is not
what fraction into which you will divide the child, one half,
one quarter . . . it's still *dead*, but . . . (*Pause.*) See how you're
listening to me? I like that. When I'm not at work, I miss it.
(*He starts to cry.*) But what are one man's sufferings? In this
shithole we call life. Where where whole *populations* . . .

Defence Attorney   Your Honor . . . ?

Judge   . . . have to boil their water. (*Slight pause.*) What?

Defence Attorney   Your Honor, if I may, that is the
subject which brings us before the Court.

Prosecutor   Your Honor, I should like to respond.

Judge   Go ahead.

Prosecutor   Your Honor, if I may. We 'do', as the court
put it, neither more or less than the heterosexuals. With as
much right. Under the law. To privacy, to dignity, to . . .

Judge   And then you watch black and white films, right?

Pause.

Prosecutor   Your Honor . . .

Judge   What is it offends you in the color process?

Defence Attorney   Your Honor, the representatives of
Two Great Peoples . . .

Prosecutor   Your Honor, it is not the color process *per se*,
but the decay of storytelling, generally acknowledged as
concurrent with, though not occasioned by the introduction
of color.

Judge   Is that so?

Defence Attorney   Your Honor, Your Honor?

Judge   What?

Defence Attorney   Your Honor, we have an infallible plan
to bring Peace to the Middle East.

Prosecutor   There are fine, *fine* color films.

Bailiff   *Drums Along the Mohawk* . . .

Judge   I saw that film. It has a lot of Indians.

Defence Attorney   Indeed it does, Your Honor.

Judge   And that illustrates my point. That *people* . . . what was I saying – ?

Prosecutor   Your Honor, I can see the Court is tired, and if I may suggest it . . .

Judge   Shakespeare was a *Jew*?

Bailiff   *And* a fag . . .

Prosecutor   You ought to know . . .

Bailiff   Excuse me?

Prosecutor   Who mentioned *Drums Along the Mohawk* . . .

Bailiff   I saw it on the airplane . . .

Prosecutor   Where? To Fire Island . . . ?

All (*gently*)   Ooooh . . .

Phone rings.

Bailiff   No, if you must know, to Ibiza . . .

Prosecutor (*into phone*)   Don't call me here.

Defence Attorney   Your Honor . . .

Prosecutor (*into phone*)   I did *not* burn the pan. And I did *not* burn the pot roast. And I am at work.

Defence Attorney   Your Honor . . .

Judge   Abraham *Lincoln* was a Jew . . .

Bailiff   He was . . . ?

Judge   Look at his *photographs*.

Defence Attorney Your Honor, the Leaders of Two Middle Eastern . . .

Judge Don't interrupt me, boyo. Do you know what I can *do*? *I* didn't know what I could do until they stuck me here . . . What do *I* know . . . ? 'Danny: how'd you like to be a Judge?' 'Sure. What's it entail . . . ?' Sitting up here, reading *National Geographic*. 'I get *bored*? Go to jail.' You think I'm kidding . . . ?

Defendant No.

Judge No, what?

Defendant No, Your Honor.

Judge I said, 'I can send 'em to jail . . . ?' 'You bet your ass.' 'Mickey,' I said, 'For *what*?' 'Anything, Dan. Anything, or nothing.' First time, did it feel funny? *Sure*. Like anything. You get used to it. Like sex. You get married. 'I can get it any time.' Weeks pass, you *realize*: there have to be *rules*. A pattern, perhaps, give and take. Sometimes she's tired . . . The things, what are they called . . . ?

Prosecutor 'Precedents'?

Phone rings.

Judge *Vibrators*. They aren't called *precedents*. Huh? Are you *fucking* with me?

Prosecutor (*into phone*)   *What?*

Defendant Your . . .

Judge What would a 'precedent' be doing in your bedside table?

Pause.

Defence Attorney Your Honor . . .

Judge *Is* there a limit on my power? Pal? You don't want to know.

Prosecutor Your Honor, I have a family situation . . .

Judge   First time I have a mother and her kid. Dad didn't want to pay child support. The mother starts to cry. A more experienced man would have imposed some, some, what are they called . . . ?

Bailiff   Judicial penalty.

Judge   Hey, *you* should be doing this job. On the *guy*. I sent the *kid* to jail.

Prosecutor   For *what*?

Judge   I don't need a *reason*; all's I need's, this little *hammer* here . . . N' I'm gonna use it till the batteries run out. (*He looks around.*) Where is it? All day I'm thinking: what can I do next? I'm *limited*, though, see, by, uh, by . . .

Defence Attorney   . . . by the law?

Judge   Yeah, where's my little hammer. Till I learn about this . . . *What* is it?

Bailiff   Community service.

Judge   Community service. *Now* I'm like, 'Uh, find a city park, and cut the grass with your teeth' . . . 'Tie your clothes into knots, and stuff 'em down the toilet.' Uh . . . 'Shove a *tomato* up your ass', uh . . .

Defendant   How would that benefit the community?

Pause.

Judge   You're kidding.

Defendant   No.

Pause.

Judge   While the offender is so engaged, is he out exposing himself to schoolchildren . . . ?

Defendant   No.

Judge   Then shut the fuck up.

Prosecutor   Begging the Court's pardon.

Judge   Fuck you, you little suck-ass. What do you say to that?

Prosecutor   Your Honor . . . (*Hangs up phone.*) A pressing, a *pressing* familial need, Your Honor, *forces* me to *ask* Your Honor if we could return to the pro . . .

Judge   And they're called *vibrators. I* oughtta know.

Defence Attorney   Your Honor. We have a plan to bring peace to the Middle East.

Judge   My God, man. Why haven't you spoke up?

Defence Attorney   We have here a method, arrived at by my client . . .

Judge   Do you think I'm made of stone?

Defence Attorney   The representatives of Two Great Powers . . .

Judge   Do you think one little comment at the nineteenth hole *disqualifies* me from feeling for the poor Jews? The poor persecuted Jews and Arabs?

Prosecutor   Your . . .

Judge   . . . who slog it out in heat and in *humidity* we civilized white folk cannot *imagine* . . . ?

Prosecutor   Your . . .

Judge   *Fuck* that. *Yes.* The white race is unsuited, yes, to labor in that equatorial heat. God, in his mercy, assigned *this* people to *rule* and that to *work.* The darkies, in the field, bent over, singing, swinging their hips in that rhythmic . . . that . . . that . . .

Bailiff   Your Honor . . .

Judge   You know what, I want to confess . . .

Bailiff   Your Honor, may I . . .

Judge   Gimme my pills.

Bailiff Your Honor, may I have those, please . . . ? (*He takes the pills.*)

Judge I want to confess.

Bailiff Your Honor, the listed side effects for your prescription . . .

Judge Fuck that into a cocked hat. I want to confess.

Bailiff Court is adjourned . . .

Judge Unh *uh*, unh *uh*.

Bailiff Your Honor . . .

Judge Everyone else gets to confess. You guilty, guilty scum. 'The dog ate my homework.' 'I had a Twinkie, that's why I shot the Pope.' What fucking bullshit. And I am forced, in the name of a 'paycheck', to, to feed my 'little ones', Lil Mickey, Lil Sue. Susie? What did I do? Susie I, I was *drunk*. That ever happen to you? One night. I swear to God one night. Two nights, at most. Susie? I didn't think that you'd *remember*.

Bailiff Court is adjourned . . .

The **Bailiff** *starts to lead the* **Judge** *away.*

Judge Do kids remember that far back?

Bailiff Your Honor . . .

Judge *Do* they? *I* don't know. I'm asking. Anybody have kids?

Prosecutor I . . .

Judge I just can't take the burden any more. What am I . . . *Switzerland*? A country with no *feelings* . . . ? You think that I don't have feelings? What do you think, I'm made of curds and whey? I'm flesh and blood, like any other man. Look, look, look, if you *cut* me, do I not bleed? Gimme that letter-opener.

The **Bailiff** *succeeds in hustling the* **Judge** *out of the chamber.*

Bailiff Short recess . . .

Pause.

Prosecutor Well. It seems . . .

The **Judge** *comes back into the courtroom, the* **Bailiff** *behind him.*

Bailiff All rise.

Defence Attorney Your, Honor, my client and I . . .

Judge Do you know, I once had an affair, with the only
ugly girl in Iceland . . . ? (*Pause.*) Now, you say, 'How Ugly
was she . . . ?'

Pause.

All How ugly was she . . . ?

Judge How ugly do you think she was?

Defence Attorney Your Honor. (*He reads from his petition.*)
'How can the unitary be divided? How can the sundered be
conjoined . . . ? Through fluid, dynamic stasis . . .

Defendant . . . brought about . . .

Defence Attorney . . . through rationalization of the
ligatures and, thus, the osteoporotic stem of life . . .

Defendant . . . the spine . . .

Defence Attorney . . . thus conducing . . .

Defendant Yes . . .

Defence Attorney . . . to peace. Christ's brilliance . . .

Judge 'Jesus' Christ?

Defendant I thought that we weren't going to put that in?

Defence Attorney No, we agreed.

Judge '*Jesus*' Christ . . . ?

Defence Attorney Well, yes. Yes. Your Honor? We have
a petition . . .

Defendant   I thought you were going to take that out . . .

Defence Attorney   If Your Honor would consent, merely, *merely*, to release us, for − (*Checks his watch.*) the next half hour, we, Christian and Jew, have a method . . .

Judge   'No no no, I will not let you go.' Who said that? *Anybody* . . . ?

Prosecutor   Pharoah.

Judge   I'm gonna take my clothes off.

He starts to do so. The **Bailiff** *tries to restrain him.*

Bailiff   Your Honor . . .

Defence Attorney   Your Honor . . .

Judge   What . . . ?

Defence Attorney   Christ's brilliance, Christ's brilliance, Your Honor, like that of Moses, like that of the Prophet . . .

Judge   The Prophet.

Defence Attorney   Mohammed.

Judge   Mohammed. The Prophet of Islam.

Defence Attorney   That's right.

Judge (*now stripped down to his undershirt*)   Whoa, whoa, whoa, then, let's be Very Careful what we say about them.

Pause.

Defence Attorney   Their teachings . . .

Judge   Hold on, let's slow it *down*: The the the, the people we're *talking* about . . .

Defence Attorney   Yes.

Judge   With the 'things' . . . around their head . . .

Defence Attorney   Yes . . .

Judge   Their 'teachings' . . .

Prosecutor　Ancient, *ancient* religion . . .

Defence Attorney　. . . consist in a message of peace.

Pause.

Judge　I don't think they can object to that, can they?

Defence Attorney　Your Honor, no.

Pause.

Judge　Those, fine, fine people . . .

Defence Attorney　Um . . .

Judge　Because I'd hate to tick them off.

Prosecutor　I'm with you *there*, Your Honor.

Judge　And I'm not just saying that because they have all the oil . . .

Prosecutor　No.

Defendant　No.

Defence Attorney　No.

Prosecutor　No indeed.

Defence Attorney　Those wonderful people . . .

Judge　But because, uh, uh . . .

Pause.

Prosecutor　Because of their 'contributions'.

Judge　Boy, you've got it there . . .

Defendant　That's for sure.

Bailiff　I love the integrity of their native textiles.

Defence Attorney　And their teachings . . .

Judge　Uh huh . . .

Defence Attorney　. . . consist, as I have said, in a message of peace.

Judge You're goddamn right they do. But what does it mean, when little children have to go to sleep every night, in garments which are too tight, revealing the various curves of their body to anybody with the least little bit of curiosity?

Defence Attorney Your Honor . . .

Judge Would you address yourself to that?

Defence Attorney Your Honor, we can bring peace to the Middle East.

Judge Is this a 'test'?

Defence Attorney No, Your Honor. It's true.

Judge How you gonna do it?

Defence Attorney My client believes that the imbalance in their countries, as reflected in their leaders, can be rectified by a readjustment of . . .

Judge You want to bring peace to the Middle East.

Defendant Yes, Your Honor.

Judge Whoa. Whoa. That's a big one. And I would *hate* to be the guy who stood in your way. Those two, what, benighted peoples, warring . . . the Curse of War brought upon them by . . . uh . . . How seldom is it given to us? (*Pause.*) May I have a hanky? (*He weeps.*)

Defence Attorney Your Honor.

Judge You wanna go lay your plan for peace, at the feet of those warring powers –

Defence Attorney No, Your Honor, we want to manipulate their neck.

Judge Sounds good to *me.*

Defence Attorney Your Honor, then yes, only, if you would . . .

Judge By Jove, I will then, by the power vested in me . . .

Defence Attorney   Your Honor, we . . .

Judge   Yes. I'm getting to it. I want to use the correct *'form'*. Order a car. I want a police car and escort to take these two gentlemen to present their petition to the Peace Conference. And now: by the power vested in me, yes to exercise compassion, it gives me great pleasure, to, as per my judicial prerogative, and for the purposes of world peace, to release the . . .

Bernard (*enters with a large suitcase. Unable to see, addresses the air*)   YOU LYING SWINE. I WAS WAITING AT *YOUR* MOTHER'S ALL YESTERDAY EVENING. THE QUICHE IS COLD, THE CAPRESE SALAD'S HOT, SHE AND I HAVE, AS YOU KNOW, NOTHING IN COMMON SAVE OUR HISTORY OF BABYING *YOU*, YOU, DECEITFUL, FORGETFUL, FAT, SLOVENLY . . .

Judge   Who is he talking to . . . ?

Bernard   . . . UNGRATEFUL . . .

Judge   . . . 'cause, if he's talking to me, that's contempt.

Bernard   . . . *OLD* . . .

Judge   I'm *sure* of that . . .

Bernard   WHERE *IS* HE? WHERE *IS* HE?

Prosecutor   Put your contacts in.

Bernard   Where *is* he?

Prosecutor   *Put your contacts in.*

Bernard   I cannot 'put my contacts in' as I have been weeping a river of tears and they will not 'go' in.

Prosecutor   Bunny . . .

Judge   Did you say you wanted to 'crick their *neck*'?

Bernard   And now I'm weeping in front of your friends. Perhaps you'd introduce me . . .

Prosecutor   I . . .

Bernard   . . . or are you ashamed of me . . . ? You ashamed of me in front of your straight friends? 'Oh, Honey . . . did you *come* yet . . . ?'

Judge   What's wrong with asking that?

Bernard   If you have to *ask* . . .

Judge   I always thought it was *polite* . . .

Bernard   Of course you did. (*To* **Prosecutor**.) And you might ask: what is this? *This* is a *suitcase*. What's in it, you wonder . . .

Prosecutor   Bernard . . .

Bernard   Oooh, our *life* together . . . oh . . .

Prosecutor   Bernard . . .

Bernard   You wouldn't even take my *call* . . .

Prosecutor   I'm trying a *case*.

Bernard   Oh, bullshit.

Prosecutor   I'm trying a *case, can't you see that*?

Bernard   Don't you use that tone with me.

Prosecutor   Buns . . .

Bernard   Don't you Buns me, you . . . you . . . Words fail me . . . *I* don't know. You try to be a *helpmate*. You try to care . . . you hope there is a God. Who sees you . . . who . . .

He dissolves in tears. Pause.

Defence Attorney   Your Honor. There exists, today only, the, perhaps the last best hope to bring peace to the Middle East. My client and I, though of different faiths . . .

Bernard   OH, FUCK *YOU*. HOW CAN YOU HAVE PEACE IN THE MIDDLE EAST WHEN YOU CAN'T HAVE PEACE IN YOUR *HOME* . . .

Judge   You know, you're right . . .

Bernard (*pointing at* **Prosecutor**) Tell *him* that. Tell him.
He's the one that should be on trial . . .

Prosecutor Bunny . . .

Bernard He *abused* me, he was *cruel* to me, and then,
when I went home to *mother*, what was his responsibility?

Judge *and* **Defendant** *and* **Defence Attorney** To come
after you.

Bernard You're goddamn *right*, to COME AFTER ME,
which is the one, *inviolable* law.

Judge He's right.

Bernard In anticipation of which, I made a quiche, a
quiche offering. When *he* was in the wrong.

Judge Huh.

Bernard AND IT'S *HIS* GODDAM *MOTHER.*

All mumble.

Judge (*to* **Prosecutor**) That's some fella you've got yourself
then . . .

Bernard I want to make a complaint, Your Honor . . .

Judge This is the most irregular . . .

Bernard I ACCUSE . . .

Holds up the legal pad he has pulled from his suitcase.

Judge . . . but-what-the-hell . . .

Bernard *I ACCUSE THAT MAN* OF . . . (*He consults his
legal pad.*)

Prosecutor Bunny, I'm trying to *work* here . . .

Bernard . . . of boorishness. (*Peers at the pad.*)

Prosecutor Bun . . .

Bernard I'm not done . . .

Judge *hands* **Bernard** *his reading glasses.*

Bernard   And a lack of sensitivity.

Judge (*to* **Prosecutor**)   If this is true, you have a *lot* to answer for . . .

Prosecutor   Your Honor . . .

Judge   To have the love of a fine young man . . .

Bernard   Thank you, Your Honor . . .

Judge   And to . . . what? *What* did he do . . . ?

Bernard   He ruined the ROASTING PAN.

Takes roasting pan from suitcase. Puts it on bench.

Judge   This pan is fine.

Bernard   He ruined the *roast* . . . I cleaned it with baking soda, he ruined our evening; and he *revealed* to me the essential emptiness, not only of *our* life. But of *my* life . . .

He cries.

Judge   Come up here . . .

Bernard   No, NO, I don't deserve affection.

Judge   Sssshhhhhhsh . . .

Bernard   I deserve *nothing* . . . that's why . . . time after time . . .

Judge   Hush . . .

Bernard   What am I? A hot-water bottle . . . a trick with his name on the lease . . . (*He weeps.*)

Judge   Sshhh. Nothing's that bad . . .

Bernard   Time after time . . . Huh. Can I pick 'em . . . Your Honor?

Bailiff   You mustn't blame yourself.

Judge   *Listen* to the man.

Bernard Cook, clean, understand when he's too tired to make love . . .

Judge Sshhh.

Bernard And who is it takes care of his mother?

Pause, **Bernard** *cries some more.*

Defence Attorney Wait . . . excuse me, are they a bunch of fags . . . ?

Bernard Why, why, why, *Why* Can't There Be Peace . . . ?

Defence Attorney Are they *queer.* Is that the punchline?

Bernard *weeps.*

Judge There, there, little fella . . .

Bernard All I ever wanted was to make a *home* . . . for some *man* . . .

Judge Sshhh . . .

Defence Attorney (*generally*) *These* guys are queer as a V-neck sweater . . .

Bernard . . . wash his *clothes* . . . Each year. The waistband on his shorts gets bigger. Do *I* complain . . . ?

Defence Attorney (*to himself*) They're a bunch of *fags* . . .

Prosecutor Objection.

Bernard *weeps.*

Judge I had a dream the other night. Of a clean land, untroubled by pollution. Untroubled by strife. With liberty and with compassion for *all* its citizens. A land administered by people of good faith and self-respect, which stood as an example to the nations. Which reached out to them. And stilled their torment with aid: with food, with medicine, with love and understanding.

Defence Attorney Your Honor . . .

Judge   And then this big fat fucking *dinosaur* came by and *stomped* everybody into moosh.

Pause.

Defence Attorney   Your Honor . . .

Judge   I think he came from Japan.

Defence Attorney   There exists . . .

Judge   I *believe* his size was the result of nuclear testing.

Defence Attorney   The possibility of bringing peace to the Middle East.

Judge   But I don't remember how the dinosaur got there in the first place.

Prosecutor   He was a lizard, from the pet store. Begging Your Honor's pardon.

Judge   What was he doing in my dream?

Prosecutor   It wasn't a dream, it was a movie.

Defence Attorney   Your Honor . . .

Judge   It was a *movie?*

Prosecutor   Yes, Your Honor.

Judge   Is it hot in here, or is it just me?

Defence Attorney   Your Honor: As we speak, two great world leaders, as we speak, are, engaged in this historic conference. Having met, in good faith, we believe. To attempt to settle the strife in the Middle East. We have devised a plan, which we feel, if it could be represented to them, would bring about that blessed result.

Prosecutor   And what *is* this plan?

Defence Attorney (*to* **Defendant**)   Tell them.

Defendant *mumbles.*

Defence Attorney   Go on . . .

Defendant *mumbles. A pause.*

Defence Attorney   Your Honor, my client believes, and has demonstrated to me, how a simple readjustment of that which very well may prove to be the fifth lumbar vertebrae, may, through a decrease in the subdural mff-mff, restore mental balance to the leaders and, through them to the populace of the Middle East.

Prosecutor   Your Honor, the case before this Court . . .

Judge   I know the case before this Court. What do you think I am, deaf? I'm not deaf. (*To* **Bailiff**.) I'm not deaf, am I, because then I couldn't hear myself. (*To self.*) Mooooo . . . Mooo . . . Mooo . . .

Bailiff   Your Honor, I've taken the liberty of asking a physician . . .

Judge   The *question* is: was Shakespeare a Jew?

Prosecutor   Your Honor . . . ?

Judge   Or was he a normal human being? (*To* **Bernard**.) My golly, you smell good.

Bernard   Thank you, Your Honor.

Judge   Call me Danny . . .

Bernard   Thank you, Danny. You're a nice man.

Judge   Oh, hush. Because I want to tell you: you bring peace to the Middle East, and you're gonna look back on it as one of the proudest days of your life.

Defence Attorney   Your Honor . . .

Judge   Was Shakespeare a Jew? You go first. Whaddaya say?

Prosecutor   Your Honor, the introduction of religion, into a Court of Law . . .

Judge   Don't take that tone with me. Jeez. You can't even be civil with your *boyfriend* . . . (*Pause.*) What *did* he do?

Bernard   He made me burn the pot roast.

Judge   YOU *SWINE*. You come *in* here, with your, your highfalutin tales of peace and, all the what, the lions will lie down with the lambs. *Bullshit. Bullshit*, is what I say. Pure *bullshit*.

Prosecutor   Your Honor . . .

Judge   Because the fucking *lambs* are *already* lying down with the lambs.

Prosecutor   Your . . .

Judge   At *night time*. What are the fucking lambs gonna do? Yawn yawn, time to turn in, think I'll go bunk with the *lions*?

Bernard   No.

Judge   You're fucking A. They're *going* to lie down with the lambs. Now . . .

Prosecutor   Your Honor . . .

Judge   The *lions*, on the other hand: they're never *ever* going to lie down with the lambs. THEY'RE GOING TO EAT THEM.

Defence Attorney   Your Honor, they depart tomorrow. But for the moment, in these fleeting moments, the representatives of two great and warring powers . . .

Judge   Do you believe those sheenies and those . . . uh, uh . . .

Bailiff   . . . fine, upstanding Arabs . . .

All   Mmm.

Judge   . . . can ever stop their stupid bitching?

Prosecutor   He didn't look like a Jew in his pictures . . .

Judge   Pictures are deceiving. Did you know that Theodore Roosevelt was a Mulatto?

Defence Attorney   Your Honor, my client . . .

Judge   Your client. Yeah, yeah. What did he do? What is it? Insider trading?

Defence Attorney   Your . . .

Judge   Child molestation? *We're* all friends here . . .

Defence Attorney   Your Honor, my client has pleaded not guilty, to . . .

Judge   Well, *duh*, *I* get it. *I'm* in on the joke. I understand. All that he's got to do. Okay, *off* the record, just for the, the, the, you concur . . .

Prosecutor   Your Honor, make him say 'I'm sorry'.

Judge   You bet. Come on now.

Bernard   Would somebody help me find my contact?

Judge   Quick quick, whatever the fellow did, you have him come up here 'n' say 'I'm sorry' – then we'll save the Middle East.

Pause.

Defendant *and* **Defence Attorney** *confer.*

Defence Attorney   Your Honor, my client has asked me to forward to this Honorable Court his statement, which consists in but those two, blessed, blessed words: 'I'm sorry'.

Prosecutor   Make him *say* it.

Judge   Say it, pal.

All murmur. **Defendant** *comes forward.*

Bernard   I think that he should say it.

Defendant   I'm sorry.

Judge   I CAN'T HEAR YOU.

Defence Attorney   Speak up, please.

Defendant   I'm sorry.

Judge   That's all it takes. And now . . .

Bernard   I know that voice . . . I KNOW THAT VOICE. GEORGE BERNSTEIN? *IS THAT YOU?* IS THAT YOU, YOU SONOFABITCH?

Defendant   I, I . . .

Bernard   HOW DARE YOU COME IN HERE AND SHOW YOUR FACE?

Defence Attorney   Who is George Bernstein?

Bernard   After you hung me out to dry in Hawaii? You sonofabitch.

Prosecutor   Who is George Bernstein?

Bernard   And you gave me a false *name*?

Defendant   Bunny. Buns . . .

Bernard   Don't you Buns me. I sat in that hotel room three days, waiting for you to come back from the ice dispenser.

Defendant   Bunny. My wife . . .

Judge   Bunny . . . ?

Bernard   Eating macadamia nuts. Do you have any *notion* the amount of carbohydrates I consumed?

Defendant   Bunny, I wanted to stay, my wife . . .

Bernard   'Oh Bunny, let me take you to Hawaii . . . '

Prosecutor   . . . take You to Hawaii . . .

Judge   'Bunny'. I *know* that name . . .

Prosecutor   YOU LITTLE WHORE. HE TOOK YOU TO HAWAII? WHEN?

Bernard   Last November.

Defendant   Bunny, my wife called, she . . .

Prosecutor   You told me you were going to Atlantic City with my mother.

Bernard   I lied, I lied, alright? D'that ever happen to you?

Defence Attorney   Your Honor . . .

Prosecutor   Where did you meet him?

Bernard   Is it important?

Prosecutor   I want to know.

Bernard   The small leather goods counter at Saks.

Defence Attorney   Your Honor . . .

Bernard   He was buying an agenda.

Defence Attorney   Your Honor, for the remainder of today . . .

Prosecutor   Your Honor, I have that agenda . . .

Defence Attorney   Scant moments, during which we may bring peace to the Middle . . .

Prosecutor   Your Honor, I have that agenda in evidence, which . . . Wait wait wait wait *wait* – MY MOTHER HELPED YOU CHEAT ON ME . . . ?

Doctor *enters.*

Doctor   I'm sorry I'm late.

Judge   And who is this, now?

Doctor   Show me the bottle. How many pills did he take?

Bailiff   Your Honor, I've taken the liberty of contacting a physician . . .

Doctor   I'm sorry that I'm late, Your Honor, I was delayed by the extraordinary security precautions attendant upon the end of the Middle East Peace Conference.

Prosecutor   You and my mother . . .

Judge 'Bunny.' His name was stuck to the note on the motion. With the *au jus*.

Doctor Give me your arm, please . . .

Judge With the *au jus* of a pot roast . . .

Doctor Give me your arm, please.

Judge This is no time to get high.

Bernard My name . . . ?

Judge It said, it said . . . (*Handing up the note.*) Here. 'I want to lick you all over. Bunny.'

Doctor Give me your arm, please.

Judge I can't right now, I'm busy – We're going to bring peace to the Middle East.

Doctor How are you going to do that?

Judge We're going to crick their necks.

Defendant That is a simplified, but an essentially correct –

Doctor This man is in the throes of a drug-induced psychotomemetic fugue.

Judge And what the fuck's it to *you*?

Doctor (*to* **Bailiff**) Subdue him, please.

Defendant I don't believe he needs a shot . . .

Doctor Excuse me?

Defendant He does not need the shot.

Doctor And now you speak in what capacity?

Defendant I speak as a chiropractor.

Doctor No, seriously . . .

Defendant Are you ignorant of the fact a heightened state of mental aggravation can be lessened, without drugs, as has been known for fifteen million years, by a simple reversal of the lumbar subluxation?

Doctor Blow me.

Defendant EXCUSE MEEEE . . . ?

Doctor Subdue the patient, please . . .

Defendant 'BLOW ME?'

Doctor Oh, is it mad because it didn't get into medical school . . . ? Subdue the patient, please.

Defendant Excuse me . . . ? Excuse me . . . ? Excuse me . . . ?

The **Defendant** *crawls up over the bench and begins strangling the* **Doctor**.

Defendant Well, how about that, how about that, huh? Does that feel good . . . ?

Doctor Ow. Ow ow ow . . . (*Et cetera.*)

Defendant How about that, huh? Is that as much fun as pimping for the insurance companies?

Doctor Help . . .

Defendant Huh? Huh? And selling your soul for an ashtray?

Doctor Help . . .

Defendant With some drug company's name on it . . . ?

Judge Where's my gavel . . . ?

Doctor Help, help . . .

Judge Where's my fucking gavel . . . ?

Defendant Didn't teach you *this* in medical school, *did* they?

He kicks the **Doctor**.

Doctor Help . . .

Defendant When they gave you that stupid white coat . . .

Pause.

Bernard Wait a sss . . . (*He appeals to the* **Judge**.) Your Honor . . . ?

Judge They took my fucking gavel . . .

Defendant Cure *cancer*, you arrogant *fuck*!

Bernard (*bangs on bench with roasting pan*) Wait a second, wait a second, wait a second!

Pause.

Judge What?

Bernard The note said, 'I want to lick you all over. Bunny'?

Judge Yes.

Bernard *begins weeping.*

Judge What?

Bernard That is the note . . . that is the note I wrote him, after our First Date. (*To* **Prosecutor**.) You *kept* it . . . ?

Prosecutor I've carried it. All this time. In my pocket.

Bernard No . . .

Prosecutor (*starting to cry*) Yes . . .

Bernard All this *time*?

Prosecutor That's right.

Bernard Oh, I've been *so* wrong . . .

Prosecutor Bunny . . .

Bernard Can you *forgive* me . . .

Prosecutor Bunny, in many ways, it's I who should beg *your* forgiveness . . .

Bernard No, no . . .

Prosecutor If I'd been more *attentive* . . .

Bernard No, no, you have your work. I *see* that, now.

Prosecutor But, Bunny. But, but I lost a sense of *balance.*

Bernard No, no, no, no, no . . .

They embrace.

Judge You see? This, *this* is what I live for. This is my dream. This is the dream of a young jurist. Not the 'bribes', not the yes, yes, we 'take' them, but what do we live for? The, the, uh, uh . . .

Prosecutor I want to dwell in peace with you for ever.

Bernard Shhh . . .

Prosecutor But I can't live in peace with this on my soul.

Bernard Tell me, and be forgiven.

Prosecutor *whispers to* **Bernard**.

Bernard I *knew.*

Prosecutor What?

Bernard I knew *ALL THE TIME* . . .

Bailiff *What*?

Pause.

Prosecutor Oh Bunny, how could I deserve you, you . . .

They weep.

Doctor I want to confess . . . I want to confess . . .

Prosecutor Oh, Bunny . . .

Doctor Once, with a female patient . . .

Defendant *I* want to confess . . . I'm *guilty* . . . *guilty*, do you hear . . . Your Honor, I'm guilty as charged.

Bernard What is he accused of?

Pause.

Defendant I attacked a chiropodist.

All murmur.

And . . .

Pause.

Prosecutor Get if off your chest.

Defendant And I had sex with a goose. (*He weeps.*)

Defence Attorney I cheated on my income tax . . .

Prosecutor I never took the bar exam . . .

Judge *I'm Jewish.*

Pause.

Doctor This man's in *shock* . . .

Judge I'm Jewish. My father told me. He confessed.

Prosecutor Oh, Your Honor . . .

Judge He came over from Poland. He told everybody he was Welsh. He was a *Jew* . . . My father was a Jew . . . I'm a Jew . . . I'm a sheeny . . . (*He weeps.*)

Defendant You're not a Jew unless your mother was a Jew.

Judge What?

Defendant You're not a Jew unless your mother was a Jew.

Judge I'm *not* a Jew . . . ?

Defendant No.

Judge (*pause*) Thank you, God. You do exist. There is a God . . . People? People, there is a God.

Doctor Hold him, while I administer the hypodermic.

Judge There is a God. It's all true. God *exists*. (*To* **Bailiff**.) Do you hear? God exists!

He goes to embrace the **Bailiff**.

Bailiff (*consoling him*)   Hush . . .

Doctor (*administering the hypodermic*)   The antidote should take effect immediately.

Judge   God exists. How could we *e'er* repay his Endless Mercies?

Defence Attorney   Your Honor, we could bring peace to the Middle East.

Bailiff   Your Honor, the car is waiting. I have called ahead, the car is waiting to transport us to the Peace Conference.

All start towards the door, save the **Judge**. *They look back and see the* **Judge** *still seated.*

Bailiff   Wait, he has to say 'Court is adjourned' . . .

Judge   Yeah, that's right, I have to, um . . .

Phone rings.

All look around to find the culprit guilty of leaving on the ringer. **Bernard** *takes the phone from his pocket.*

Bernard   Hello . . . ?

Defendant   If Your Honor will but say 'Court is adjourned' . . .

Bernard (*apologizing to Court, as he opens his phone*)   I'm sorry . . . (*To* **Prosecutor**.) It's your mother.

Prosecutor   I have nothing to say to her.

Bernard   She wants to know if you're watching the Peace Conference on TV.

Prosecutor   Tell her I can't talk now. I'm *working*.

Bernard   Mom? Mom? He's working . . . ?

Defence Attorney   If Your Honor will but say, 'Court is adjourned'.

Bernard (*reiterating the question of the* **Prosecutor**'s *mother*)
'Did you hear what the one fellow called the other fellow at
the Peace Conference . . . ?' *What?* He called the other guy
what . . . ? On TV . . . ?

Defendant   What, what did he say?

Bernard   Can I repeat it in a Court of Law . . . ? He
said . . .

Sounds of sirens. All listen.

Judge   Would somebody turn off the kettle . . . ?

Bailiff   Your Honor, that is the sounds of sirens.

Defence Attorney   The leaders have quitted the Peace
Conference. They have departed in wrath.

Defendant   Our hopes for peace are dashed. Once again
we are Too Late. (*Collapses in chair.*)

Judge   Where am I . . . ?

Doctor   I've brought him out too quickly.

Judge   Why am I in my underwear?

Doctor   Can you say your name . . . ?

Judge   I . . .

Doctor   What do you call this little hammer . . . ?

Judge   Uh . . .

Doctor   Is there anything you know for sure?

Judge   I know . . . I know . . . I know a paste of equal
parts water and baking soda will soak a roasting pan clean
overnight.

Bailiff   But, what?

Judge *and* **Bailiff**   But never use it on a copper pan.

Bailiff (*putting his hand on the* **Judge**)   And, yes, we may
have spent our vacation on Ibiza, but we were on the *straight*
part of the island.

All   Oh, *please* . . .

Defendant   Too late, too late . . . why, Lord, oh why are we doomed to endless strife?

Defence Attorney   Well, everything was going fine till you killed Christ.

General dispproval. **Defendant** *gets incensed.*

Judge   Hey, in all fairness, he's right. But that's a question for another day. (*Bangs gavel.*) Next case.